Diwali in India

Donna Bailey and Malcolm Rodgers

M

MACMILLAN EDUCATION

One of the most important Hindu festivals
is the festival of Diwali.
This takes place in late October or
early November when the moonless nights
are very dark.

2

Diwali is a time when everyone in
the family tries to get together.
But first people get their houses ready
for the festival.
In the weeks before Diwali everybody
is busy cleaning and decorating their homes.

In some houses the women make
beautiful patterns on their floors
with coloured rice-flour paste.
There are many different patterns.

People make these patterns to ask for
the blessing of the goddess Lakshmi.
Lakshmi visits the houses at Diwali and
brings good luck for the coming year.

Some families set up a small shrine
to Lakshmi in their homes.
They put decorations, flowers and candles
around a statue of Lakshmi.

People buy garlands of fresh flowers
to decorate their statues of Lakshmi.
They also decorate the entrances to
their shops and homes.

Diwali lasts from three to five days.
During this time hundreds of lights are lit
at dusk in all the towns and villages
throughout India.

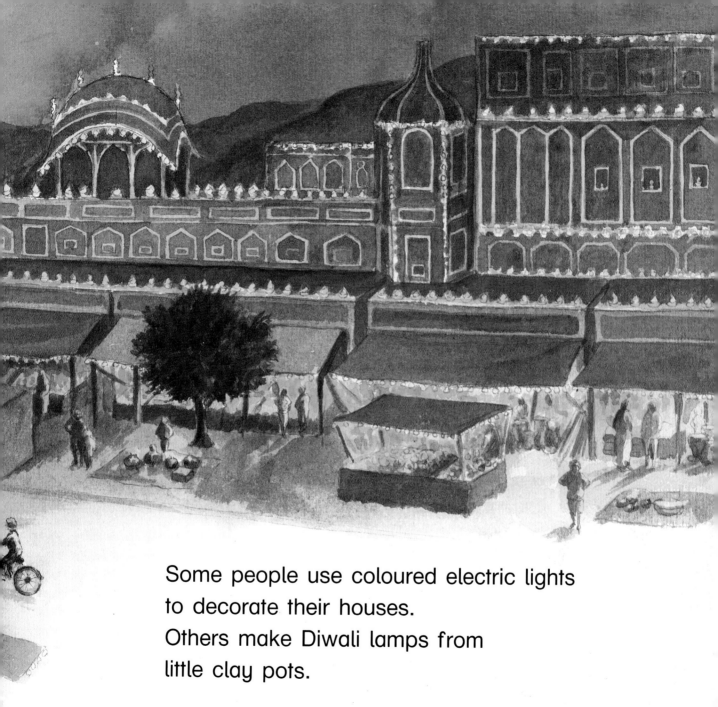

Some people use coloured electric lights
to decorate their houses.
Others make Diwali lamps from
little clay pots.

9

They fill the lamps with oil
and light the floating wicks.
People put their Diwali lights on
every ledge and shelf, both inside and
outside their homes.

Before Diwali people buy new clothes.
The women wear their best saris and
put flowers and perfume in their hair.
They buy lots of coloured bracelets
to match their new clothes.

During Diwali every town and village has a fair.
Crowds of people come from all around.
There are side shows and fair wheels to ride on.

There are stalls where people can buy
hot spicy food or sweets and sticky snacks.
The sweets are made from
boiled milk and sugar.
They are flavoured with nuts,
fruits and raisins.

At some stalls the women can have
beautiful patterns painted on their hands.
The patterns are painted in a brown dye
called henna.

Acrobats, snake charmers and jugglers
entertain the crowds at the fair.
There is also lots of music and dancing.
In the evening there are firework displays.

Index